EVERYBODY'S SOMEBODY!

By **ROGER BRADFIELD**
with Dooley
and his friends

A Division of G/L Publications **G/L REGAL BOOKS** Glendale, California, U.S.A.

To Bob Van Kampen,
who showed me the way.

Other good Regal reading:
  Living It Up by Jack Wiens
  Benjamin Alexander Sheep by Bob Friedman
  Kid Stuff Eleanor L. Doan, editor
  Guide to Ecclesiastical Bird Watching
    by LeRoy Koopman
  Sacred Cows Make Good Hamburgers by James C. Hefley

© Copyright 1977 by G/L Publications
All rights reserved

Published by Regal Books Division, G/L Publications
Glendale, California 91209
Printed in U.S.A.

Library of Congress Catalog Card No. 77-73180
ISBN 0-8307-0533-3

INTRODUCTION

I have been writing—and drawing—"Dooley's World" each day now for about five years. Relatively new, and certainly not one of the "big" strips like "Peanuts" or "Blondie," it *is* syndicated in cities from Buffalo, New York to Sydney, Australia, and reaches into several million homes.

An audience this size, seven days a week, affords one a most unusual opportunity for a bit of Christian witnessing. As a Christian, I think I am obliged to take advantage of that fact.

Certainly a comic strip is not a proper forum for preaching (for one thing, neither readers or newspaper editors would stand for it) but I feel strongly that if I can show that my characters have a belief in God and His values, a Christian message will somehow shine through. Happily, my mail indicates that a surprising number of readers sense that "Dooley's World" is written by a Christian who tries to impart a subtle Christian flavor to his strip.

Since it is important to be familiar with the characters in any book we read (be it the Bible or a lowly comic book), let me give a brief description of the characters who appear on the following pages.

Max the mouse is a tender little soul. He is naive and trusting and, as a result, often is taken advantage of. He plays the "mouse organ," but not very well.

The Professor, a wind-up toy, is a consummate blowhard. He spews forth a constant stream of misinformation—like the time he explained to Dooley that the leaning tower of Pisa is actually just an optical illusion. The tower, he explained, is perpendicular, but the entire town of Pisa is tilted. "The natives," he said, "capitalize on the illusion to attract tourists to their PISA PARLORS."

Another wind-up toy is Norman, the little tin knight. A little more worldly and knowledgeable than the others, he usually makes a lot more sense; hence his role is that of a straightman.

O'l belligerent Thelma, a rather scruffy rag doll, is coarse and loud and self-centered. An avid women's libber, she objects loudly to the fact that in church "All they ever sing are 'hymns'—never 'hyrs'!"

Dooley himself is about seven years old. He believes everything the Professor tells him and as a result will never graduate from second grade. He is continually awed by God's many miracles—they boggle his mind. But, then, he readily admits his mind "has a low boggle-point."

I thank my wife Joan (who has an incredibly *high* boggle-point) for her encouragement and patience, and for her valuable help in selecting the Bible quotations appearing in the text.

This prayer is a *rerun*? And why not? A Christian prays repeatedly for things—sometimes over a period of years. After all, praying to God is not like rubbing a genie from a lamp and being granted three wishes. Praying is talking to our Lord—a Lord who always listens, but, in His wisdom, may or may not answer immediately or even in the way we would imagine He should.

In the same way, a wise parent does not always accede to the wishes of his offspring. He may want very much to give his child that bicycle he's been asking for, but if that child is only four years old, the parent knows he isn't ready for it.

Prayer is not some sort of theological Aladdin's lamp. It is a dialogue with our Maker. We are letting Him know our immediate wants, our concerns, our hopes for the future. We are expressing thanks for His love and for His abundant blessings.

Dooley has a childlike faith in the Lord and in prayer. He has no doubts that he is being heard and, what's more, that the Lord is giving him His full attention and is considering his request. Even if Dooley should (heaven forbid!) fail his next arithmetic test, it would not signal an end or a weakening of his faith.

This prayer, a rerun? Let's hope so. Let's hope we have enough faith in prayer to sponsor a lifetime of reruns.

"Continue steadfastly in prayer, being watchful in it with thanksgiving"
(Col. 4:2).

8

Unfortunately, there are lots of folks who confuse knowing *things* about the church with religion. They know a narthex from a chancel, and a chasuble from an acolyte, but they don't know the joy of letting Christ into their hearts.

They can quote Bible verses for every occasion and recite by heart long passages from both Old and New Testaments, and yet they are not students of God's Word.

So many good souls spend lifetimes at the church preparing potluck suppers—serving on committees, organizing benefits for the needy—and confuse these activities (worthwhile as they may be) with involvement in the real purpose of the Church—the giving over of our lives to Christ.

We don't enter the kingdom of heaven by good works but by faith. It follows logically that through faith we are led to works that benefit our church, our brothers, and our community.

"For by grace are ye saved through faith;
and that not of yourselves: it is the gift of God: not of works,
lest any man should boast" (Eph. 2:8,9, KJV).

The Lord, of course, does not have technical difficulties. With Him all things are possible. Miracles happen every day, every minute, every second. Is not the opening of a flower to the sun a miracle? Or the development of a Paderewski (or a Hank Aaron, or the lady next door) from a seed too small to be seen?

Keeping snow off a driveway hardly compares with the creation of a sunset, or of the sun itself, or of a universe! But God has physical laws as well as spiritual laws. Snow that falls on our lawn necessarily falls also on our driveways; forks knocked off the table fall down—not up; and the world keeps spinning at a divinely predetermined rate, traveling at exactly the right speed in a perfect orbit.

By merely observing the marvels inherent in one tiny finger of a baby's hand—its ability to sense heat, cold, pain, its capacity to move, the master plan of bone, muscle, nerve and skin—we must admit that miracles are commonplace to the Lord.

"For in him all things were created, in heaven and on earth . . . all things were created through him and for him" (Col. 1:16).

12-24
BRADFIELD

Readers of the comic strip "Dooley's World" know that Thelma is a belligerent, self-centered, and sometimes violent character.

She believes, she says, in "the grand old concept of might makes right." She will write to Santa "only if he'll send a stamped, self-addressed envelope."

Unfortunately, the world is crowded with characters like Thelma. They run roughshod over others, concerned only with their own well-being and oblivious to the wants and/or rights of others. We must realize, however, that inside each Thelma is a voice crying out for love. It's not a loud voice, but if we listen long enough and intently enough we will hear it.

Some of us ask loudly and clearly for love. We want it, cherish it and revel in it. Others, like Thelma, won't admit they need anything that they themselves cannot supply. But deep inside something is missing. And deep inside they know it!

God loves the Thelmas of this world just as much as He loves His most faithful servants; He extends His gifts to all without qualification.

"Little children, let us stop just saying we love people; let us really love them, and show it by our actions" (1 John 3:18, TLB).

Another example of misdirected "Bible study." Students over the centuries have compiled every imaginable statistic from both the Old and New Testaments. Some have recorded, as Thelma discovers, how many times certain words appear, or how many references are made in each chapter to certain events or places. Some have devised involved mathematical formulas that "prove" the divine origin of the Bible because of the way certain words or letters appear in patterns (forgetting, perhaps, how the original books have been translated). The Bible emerges as some sort of magician's handbook—a sorcerer's tool that, when rubbed three times, will yield its magic.

In their zeal, these scholars confuse "studying the Bible" with studying the message of the Bible, the message of God's promises to man as set down over the ages through divine inspiration.

"Study to show thyself approved unto God, a workman that needeth not to be ashamed, rightly dividing the word of truth" (2 Tim. 2:15, KJV).

Of the billions of people who have trod this globe since Adam, not one has "gotten his day back." The combined riches of Solomon, Faisal and Onassis couldn't purchase one millisecond of time—it races on at exactly sixty minutes per hour night and day, and will forever.

How we spend this time is of prime importance. Why, then, is the world crowded with folks who consult bankers and lawyers and investment counselors before buying a stock, yet squander their time as though they had an endless supply?

The ways we spend time are more numerous and varied than the ways we spend money. We can spend it doing God's will, denying Him, ignoring Him. We can spend it loving or hating, sniffing God's flowers or Mr. DuPont's glue, writing a sonnet or a ransom note. Once the time is spent, though, that's it. God provides no sales slip to bring back for exchanges.

Instead of complaining, Thelma-like, about our "rotten days," we would do better to count our endless blessings: our health, our abundance of food, our friends and families, the gift of life itself bestowed by an ever-loving Creator.

Since we have only one chance at our day, we should live it as though it is our last. Or at least spend it with full knowledge of its worth!

"This is the day which the Lord has made; let us rejoice and be glad in it" (Ps. 118:24).

"I read about it in a book" I wonder how many readers of this Sunday page stopped to think about which book Max was referring to?

To Christians, the message is obvious. The primary source for learning about the power of love is the Bible. The power of love is stronger than any other, yet millions of our citizens turn to other books that tell us we can solve our problems through positive thinking, proper diet, meditation, proper sexual techniques, or even by letting the stars direct our actions.

The truth is, we solve our problems by giving them to God—by letting Him come into our lives and TAKE OVER. The words "take over" are important. Too often we invite the Lord on our life journey then relegate Him to a spot in the back seat. Rather than inviting Him up front to do the driving, we expect Him to be "on call" like some sort of private mechanic who's summoned into action only at times of carburetor or ignition trouble.

God's first commandment is:

"And he said to him, 'You shall love the Lord your God with all your heart, and with all your soul, and with all your mind'" (Matt. 22:37).

In Luke 12:6,7 we read: "Are not five sparrows sold for two farthings, and not one of them is forgotten before God? But even the very hairs of your head are all numbered. Fear not therefore: ye are of more value than many sparrows" (*KJV*).

If we believe that statement, if we believe that we are not something less than birds, we must also believe that God does not confine His love to "mankind" or "people" or "nations." He knows and loves YOU and ME as *individuals.* He knows our wants, our wishes, and what the future holds for us.

The mere fact that it is beyond our capacity to comprehend how a Superior Being can keep track of several billion souls on an individual and constant basis does not preclude that fact's existence. We cannot comprehend the vastness of the universe, but the universe exists. We cannot explain life, but that, too, exists. We may not comprehend God's love for each one of us, but it is always available.

It is an exhilarating thing to realize that God loves us on an individual basis. He awaits each of us with open arms, ready to accept us, to love us, and to forgive our sins for all eternity.

Yes, Max. Everybody's somebody!

"The same Lord is Lord of all and bestows his riches upon all who call upon him" (Rom. 10:12).

28

Here again, we have an example of the power of love, the power that can easily turn a plain rock into an object of great value.

Almost every parent has received crudely (but lovingly) wrapped presents of paperweights, paper bookmarks, handprints in clay, and out-of-round bowls (or are they cups without handles?). The inestimable value these objects have comes from the outpouring of love that goes into their making and into their *giving.*

Dooley, when asked how he could give his mother a lumpy handmade ashtray for Mother's Day (especially since she didn't smoke), replied with remarkable logic, "Mother's Day gifts aren't for using, they're for getting."

Some of us who are the very richest don't realize it because we're using our bank balance for a gauge. Our bookkeeping systems are faulty. We're taking inventory of the wrong treasure. We should be adding up our stores of love.

Maybe we've got the wrong accountant.

"Do not lay up for yourselves treasures on earth,
where moth and rust consume and where thieves break in and steal,
but lay up for yourselves treasures in heaven" (Matt. 6:19,20).

This comic strip was prepared eight or nine weeks ahead of the date on which it was due to appear in various newspapers around the country.

I chose the name "Wilson School" only by chance.

The day after the strip appeared, I received a call from an officer of the Wilson PTA thanking me for the "timely ad" and reporting that their meeting of the night before had been attended by about twice the usual number of parents.

Some might say, "Godly intervention!"

I would be inclined to say, "humorous coincidence," although never doubting the Lord's ability to act as media director for the PTA if He so chose.

As Christians, we know that God is *in charge* and that for Him all things are possible. Yet the Lord, in His wisdom, gave each of us the power to decide for ourselves what course our lives should take.

We decide whether or not to attend PTA meetings or church services or adult movies. *We* decide whether to accept the Lord or the devil—whether to accept handouts or responsibilities.

It's been said that even "deciding not to decide" is making a choice.

"In everything a prudent man acts with knowledge, but a fool flaunts his folly" (Prov. 13:16).

The poverty-stricken people of the world far out-number those of us who are blessed with comfortable homes, warm clothing and plenty to eat.

However, there is more than one way to measure "poverty." Who is truly poverty-stricken, he who goes without food or he who hungers for the Lord and knows not how to receive Him?

Almost every day we can read of wealthy, well-known, "important" people who, in spite of their fame and fortune, lead miserable lives. They divorce their spouses, shoot their lovers and sometimes themselves. They desperately seek solace in drugs and alcohol.

By any sensible measuring stick, *they* are the truly poverty-stricken. They are without life-sustaining essentials: love, compassion, belief. They are without Christ in their lives.

Unlike the starving millions throughout the world who are reduced to begging for food, those who would have Christ need not beg but merely *accept* Him.

What a joyous revelation to realize that Christ is there at our door waiting to be asked in; waiting to shoulder our burdens and dissipate our fears; waiting to envelop us in God's everlasting love.

"Real life and real living are not related to how rich we are"
(Luke 12:15, TLB*).*

34

36

Thelma won't admit, even to herself, that she's capable of shedding a tear—just as so many of us won't admit that *we* have tender spots.

How awful, though, to imagine a world entirely devoid of tenderness. What a cold, barren place that would be: no love songs written, no flowers sent, no children tucked in at night, no dogs patted or get-well cards sent. Fathers of the bride would walk down the aisle dry-eyed to give their favorite daughters away.

That's not the kind of world God wanted us to live in. Let's admit our tenderness and our weakness. If we can just bring ourselves to say, "Lord, I can be hurt. I'm vulnerable. I need your help!"

The help and love we need so desperately are there in unbelievable quantities. Just waiting.

"Hitherto you have asked nothing in my name;
ask, and you will receive, that your joy may be full" (John 16:24).

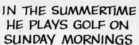

A person's religion has been defined simply as "that which interests him most." In other words, as that particular thing on which most of his energy is expended, or to which he devotes the most thought.

Are our lives centered on Christ or on our business? Do we spend more time reflecting on how Jesus would have us live or on how to swing a golf club or decorate a room? Does the hour we spend in church on Sunday represent our entire spiritual life? What about the other 167 hours each week?

I would ask those who consider themselves Christians solely by virtue of that weekly hour in church to reflect on the words of the grizzled old farmer who said, "Ya can spend an hour a week in a chicken coop, but that don't make ya no chicken!"

"Seek the Lord and his strength, seek his presence continually!"
(Ps. 105:4).

Life *doesn't* follow the script, although sometimes we wish it did. Problems continually creep into even the best regulated lives—faucets drip, batteries go dead, bursitis sets in, bills pile up.

Being a Christian doesn't assure us a trouble-free life, far from it! God loves us too much for that; just as He loved Adam so much that He gave him freedom of choice. (Yes, even freedom to choose a life of sin.)

Let's face it, we human beings arrive on earth without even a 90-day guarantee on moving parts, and we have no idea what the future holds. Why didn't God arrange things so that every day would have been perfect? He *could* have, of course.

But what's the point in running a race we can't lose? or the satisfaction in winning a fight that's "fixed"? Who wants to read a mystery when he already knows "who done it"? If it's a "sure thing," it isn't life.

While life may not follow the script, it does provide cue cards—clear instructions on how to live—in large, easy-to-read type, set down by some of the best writers of the last two thousand years: Matthew, Mark, Luke, John, Paul—

"For whatever was written in former days was written for our instruction, that by steadfastness and by the encouragement of the scriptures we might have hope" (Rom. 15:4).

MOM'S BEEN SHOPPING EVERY DAY THIS WEEK!

12-20

—AN' EVERY EVENING SHE'S BEEN WRAPPIN' PACKAGES.. MAKING FRUITCAKE... ADDRESSING CARDS—

SHE'S CERTAINLY BUSY!

YES—SHE SAYS IT'S A SHAME THEY HAVE TO HAVE CHRISTMAS RIGHT DURING THE HOLIDAYS

Christmas has come to mean, to the vast majority of us, something other than the celebration of the birth of our Lord, Jesus Christ. It has come to mean bearded men in red suits, street decorations, office parties and *gifts*—gifts for the kids, mom, dad, Aunt Martha, the minister and the postman, plus a buck extra for the delivery boy from the liquor store.

It's as if we were all invited to some huge, frantic birthday party (all of us, that is, except the one who is actually having the birthday) at which all the guests arrive loaded with gifts and then proceed to exchange them *with each other.*

Santa Claus (a lovable old gent, but nowhere mentioned in either the Old or New Testament) has become the star of the production, while Christ is relegated to a non-speaking bit part with an appearance late in the third act.

While only a Scrooge would argue that gifts are not a legitimate part of our Christmas celebration, if we would concentrate a little less on gifts to each other and turn instead to gifts of love and adoration and commitment to Christ, Christmas would regain its true meaning.

It's a BIRTHDAY PARTY!

Everyone's invited!

R.S.V.P.

"For to you is born this day, . . . a Savior, who is Christ the Lord"
(Luke 2:11).

To Max the mouse, "very truly yours" is just as fitting and respectful an ending to his prayer as "amen." Those who know Max know that his prayers are filled with *sincerity*—a far more important ingredient than "proper form."

Why, then, do we find so many congregations spending their time arguing over minor variations of the form their worship should take? How many congregations have split into opposing factions trying to decide whether communion should be celebrated with wafers or real bread; whether the choir should wear red or black robes; whether to say "forgive us our sins" rather than "forgive us our trespasses"; whether the offering should be taken before or after the sermon? And how many hours have been spent, and tempers lost, and tears shed over that great theological debate of the '60s: "Is guitar music *really* so much less pleasing to God's ear than organ music?"

The story of the Little Drummer Boy tells of a toy drum played with as much love and respect and glory as any rendition of Handel's Messiah played on the world's mightiest Wurlitzer.

When Max says "very truly yours," what he really means is "very truly YOURS."

"Don't get involved in arguing over unanswerable questions and controversial theological ideas" (Titus 3:9, TLB).

46

Thelma's just illustrated another example of giving lip service to a message—one she neither lives by nor understands.

The delight of giving is an acquired taste. We are not born with a desire to *give*. Our desires are all to *take*. At first we want to take food and shelter and comfort. Then gradually the list of wants keeps growing.

Unfortunately, the list is not limited to those things that are rightfully ours. It might include, at first, our playmate's toys, later on our schoolmate's geometry answers, and, if the trend continues, eventually our neighbor's wife. It is only after we learn to love our fellowman that we can become aware that giving can bring far more happiness than receiving.

Paradoxical as it may sound, giving is a form of receiving. As we give, we receive joy in return. As we give our lives to Christ we receive salvation in return—the best bargain any of us will ever get!

Salvation is free, not even an extra charge for handling and mailing.

The price is right.

"Give, and it will be given to you; good measure, pressed down, shaken together, running over, will be put into your lap. For the measure you give will be the measure you get back" (Luke 6:38).

If we were to make a list of the very best things in life —a oneness with Christ, love, health, family, etc.— we would see that none of these things can be bought with money so, in respect, they are free. These "best things" are gifts from God.

Everything else has a price tag. Plus tax.

Unfortunately, the maintenance of a church and the spreading of the gospel fall into this "everything else" category. Churches periodically need new roofs and modernized plumbing. Ministers and missionaries need food and clothing and homes just like the rest of us. Bibles and hymnals and tracts aren't printed for free by elves at night. They're printed in union shops on paper that costs twice as much now as it did just a couple of years ago.

Unfortunately, also, an awful lot of us pay $3.50 to get into a movie on Saturday night, then, perfectly at ease, drop only a neatly-folded dollar bill into our church's collection plate on Sunday morning.

Well, maybe not *perfectly* at ease. Collection counters will tell you that almost without exception the bills with Washington's picture are folded, while the bills featuring Lincoln and Grant are invariably laid flat.

There's a lesson in human nature there somewhere.

Take to yourselves to care for the church of God. (See Acts 20:28.)

Years ago, when I was quite young, I asked our minister a question about prayer. I was hesitant, I told him, about praying for things that weren't really important. In my book, praying for Aunt Martha's recovery from gall bladder surgery was important, while praying for success in a history test seemed relatively *un*important.

Was the Lord (who, after all, had the heavens and earth to regulate, not to mention all those souls to look after) really interested in my small day-to-day problems? Were history tests and flat tires and teen-age acne worthy of His attention?

If I was "on the line" constantly with minor requests, how would the Lord react when "something big" came along. Would I have used up my "line of credit?" Would He be inclined to say, "Oh, not *him* again!"?

Our minister, a wise old Scotsman, merely said, "You go ahead and pray all you want, lad. I think God can handle it."

Dooley, much smarter at his age than I was, relies with complete faith on the Lord *for all things*. Instead of depending on the Bureau of Emissions Control, the Army Corps of Engineers, and Smokey the Bear to control "smog, floods, and forest fires," he goes right to the top.

Dooley dials the Lord. Person to person.

"Have no anxiety about anything,
but in everything by prayer and supplication with thanksgiving let
your requests be known to God" (Phil. 4:6).

The insurance policy covering the church I attend actually does have a clause in it excluding "acts of God" from coverage.

"Acts of God," I suppose, include things not attributable to man—things like hurricanes, tornadoes, lightning and earthquakes. I'm not sure about floods. I suppose a really determined man, or group of men, could cause a flood if they put their minds to it.

Our policy *does* cover, however, things like water damage resulting from a leaking roof. Just whom does the Prudential Company think controls the rain, anyway? (Certainly not our minister, who couldn't even call it off on the afternoon of the choir picnic!)

God causes *all* things. Hecauses the rain to fall and the grass to spring up as a result. He causes the earth to revolve and the seasons to change.

When God works *through* man to accomplish some goal, man is too often inclined to take the credit for himself; to think of himself as a creator rather than a tool. It's like the paintbrush taking credit for the ceiling of the Sistine Chapel.

"O Lord, how manifold are thy works!
In wisdom hast thou made them all" (Ps. 104:24).

54

Lots of folks won't accept reality. They prefer to look at their lives and at their problems from a dozen other angles. When they encounter trouble, as they invariably do, they see themselves as victims of everything from bad luck to the position of the stars.

They fail to acknowledge Jesus Christ as the *one* reality—the one source of life and love and security. Instead they deny the reality of Christ and place their faith only in those things they can see, hold or touch. To them, these things represent reality, and they are unable to believe in a God who must be accepted by faith.

Have you ever heard religion described as "just a crutch?" Something for folks who just couldn't make it on their own? I've got news for you. None of us can make it on our own.

Not to heaven, anyway.

"Now faith is the assurance of things hoped for, the conviction of things not seen" (Heb. 11:1).

Almost everybody worries to some extent about tomorrow, but nobody worries about yesterday. There is no logical reason for this because there is exactly as much to be gained by worrying about one as about the other.

If those of us who continually worry, and thereby bring more anguish into our lives than really has to be there, would just turn those worries over to the Lord! If we would just say to Him, "Lord, I'm not capable of handling this situation. Will you take over? Will you be the guiding force in my life?"

Some time after I made my own decision to let Christ come into my life and take over, I adopted this personal motto—it's lettered on a card and tacked to the top of my drawing board: "I'd rather have the Creator of the Universe running my life than some second-rate cartoonist."

No contest there!

"Trust in the Lord with all thine heart; and lean not unto thine own understanding. In all thy ways acknowledge him, and he shall direct thy paths" (Prov. 3:5,6, KJV).

How comforting to know that we can never be "lost in the crowd" when the Lord is with us. We are continually in His sight, within His reach, and enveloped in His love.

It's beyond our intellectual capacities to understand the mechanics of *how* the Lord can be with each of us simultaneously. However, even one of Ma Bell's telephone exchanges, consisting mainly of wire and plastic, can handle an amazing number of customers simultaneously. And bill us automatically at the end of the month, to boot!

We proud humans have to realize our limitations! If all the things we don't understand were "impossible," the world would simply not exist. There would be no life because we don't understand it. There would be no gravity to hold us to the globe, no electricity, no cell-multiplication, no photosynthesis, no . . . well, the list is endless. It's endless because it's in direct ratio to our ignorance.

The Lord is our *personal* Saviour. To Him we are not numbers stacked in a computer or on an IRS form or on a magazine subscription list. We are individuals, each of whom God knows and loves.

"What is impossible with men is possible with God" (Luke 18:27).

Half the world, it seems, is on automatic pilot. Half of us go through life mechanically living each day as a carbon copy of the preceding one. It's as though some giant cookie cutter was slowly stamping out identical segments of our lives on some imperceptibly-moving production line.

This process can take place so smoothly, so rhythmically, that we don't realize what is going on until a good deal of our "cookie dough" is used up.

God gave us our days to fill with love, to live with eagerness and expectation. Each day is a gift from the Lord and we should begin it by thanking Him for it. We should use a portion of it to praise Him and a portion of it to do His work. We should end it on our knees expressing gratitude for the gift of life.

A day is not something to merely live through. It's something to *celebrate.*

"Every day I will bless thee, and praise thy name for ever and ever"
(Ps. 145:2).

Thelma writes a week in advance because of her unreasonable (and unjustified) faith in her ability to control coming events.

However, our future *was* foretold thousands of years in advance—foretold, written down and even chiseled in stone. Our Bible is full of prophecies that have come true over the centuries, unfolding before our eyes and the eyes of our forefathers in a most awesome and breathtaking way.

The birth of Christ was foretold (Isa. 7:14) some seven centuries before it happened. As far back as Genesis, God made covenants with man and his descendants. These promises are still being fulfilled, like clockwork, as history unfolds.

Even during our lifetime these prophecies continue to be fulfilled. For example, the return of the Jews to Jerusalem, foretold in Zechariah 8:7,8, came about Monday morning, June 5, 1967.

Christian prophets were flesh-and-blood men just as you and I. They chronicled, bit-by-bit, God's story, from the beginning of His creation to eternity, *by His direction.* These stories were compiled and edited by other God-directed mortals and published as the all-time best-seller: the Holy Bible.

"No prophecy ever came by the impulse of man,
but men moved by the Holy Spirit spoke from God" (2 Pet. 1:21).

68

Recognizing our faults is a big step—one that's hard to take. We have to look in the mirror and admit that the incredibly handsome image being reflected back is not without blemish. We have to admit that inside that well-shaped head we've been admiring all these years is a mind that harbors evil thoughts, has known greed and selfishness, and is no stranger to sin.

It doesn't do us much good to take that first step—recognizing our faults—unless we make an effort to take the second—*doing* something about them.

The GOOD NEWS is that we can have our sins forgiven just by coming to Christ with an open heart and accepting Him and His unqualified blessings. From this point forward we no longer have to try to change our ways alone; we have the Lord's help.

The free gift of salvation is now being offered at many convenient locations. No coupons necessary. One to a customer.

"If we confess our sins, he is faithful and just, and will forgive our sins and cleanse us from all unrighteousness" (1 John 1:9).

Nowhere in all of God's vast creation is His magnificence more clearly illustrated than in His fashioning of man. Man's brain is an electrical marvel far beyond the complexity and capacity of any computer. The mechanics of his body operate with a logical precision far beyond any engineer's ability to duplicate. And the sophistication of that body's chemistry is beyond our comprehension.

Max, the mouse, knows that if his little limb is hinged in the middle, God made it that way for a good reason and not by chance. Our elbows bend so we can get food to our mouths; our pores open and close to control our temperature; even our eyebrows have a function!

Since we have been created with such magnificent equipment and placed in such an awe-inspiring environment in which to use it, it seems only reasonable that we should live our lives praising the Lord and conducting ourselves in a manner pleasing to Him.

He doesn't ask much in return, just that we accept Him for what He is. As Thelma would say, "IS THAT ASKING TOO MUCH?"!

"O the depth of the riches and wisdom and knowledge of God!"
(Rom. 11:33).

Thelma's twisted logic seems to be, "If ya can't buy it, it can't be worth much!"

Wrong, Thelma! If you *can* buy it, it positively doesn't have any lasting value. We spend our time, our energy, our whole lives pursuing things we can *buy,* when the most valuable things are absolutely *free!*

While an impressive financial statement can be important in gaining our admission to a country club, it won't do much good in getting us into heaven. Jesus tells us (Matt. 19:24) that it's harder for a rich man to enter the kingdom of heaven than for a camel to pass through the eye of a needle. This doesn't mean the Lord begrudges us any riches; indeed, He wants us to prosper. It simply means that a wealthy man is more *likely* to be one who has directed his time and energy toward material goals rather than spiritual and has, perhaps, been subject to more temptation.

God charges no admission to His kingdom, not even a cover charge or minimum. Just be sure, though, to call ahead for a reservation.

"For we brought nothing into the world, and we cannot take anything out of the world" (1 Tim. 6:7).

75

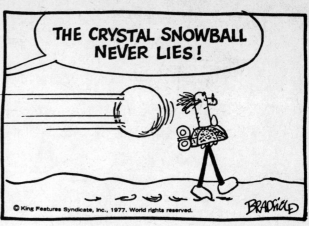

Each winter Thelma makes a "crystal snowball," and for a couple of weeks I'm provided with strip ideas while she "foretells the future" in it. (Once last year she mistakenly looked at it upside down and foretold the *past.* That was the day she predicted the victory of the Allies in World War II, the invention of the telephone, and the Yankees' 1962 World series triumph.)

Thelma puts her faith in crystal balls, tarot cards, stars, palmists and phrenologists. (Phrenologists, as you know, read bumps on people's heads. Thelma in her brief career in phrenology, used a small hammer as part of her equipment, thoughtfully providing gratis bumps for those customers lacking them.)

Countless thousands of readers turn each day to the astrology forecast in their daily newspapers. Many of them actually believe what they read there and guide their lives accordingly.

I must confess that, for a time, I too was quite fascinated by the syndicated horoscope in our paper; but then, I had my *own system* of using it: instead of looking up "my" sign (Virgo) and accepting whatever forecast I found there, I would glance through *all* the various signs and choose the prediction I liked best.

I don't suppose many astrologers would endorse my method, but, y'know, some of those forecasts *did* come true!

"So, dear friends, carefully avoid idol-worship of every kind"
(1 Cor. 10:14, TLB).

Dooley's father was right for once! He *will* eventually become obsolete, and it *was* planned that way! His earthly body will eventually stop rejuvenating itself and start its inevitable disintegration.

You and I and every other mortal will eventually wear out—it's that simple. Our bodies will return to dust in spite of the finest maintenance program, in spite of total abstinence from all known vices, in spite of who we are or whom we know.   If we know Jesus Christ, however, we need have no fear of death since through Him we will know another, more lasting life. We will have been born again to a life with a warrantee period that can't be beat—*Eternity.* (Not "eternity or 50,000 miles, whichever comes first," but eternity, period!)

This second life comes with a full, written guarantee. It's called the Bible.

Read the fine print sometime.

"All are from dust, and all turn to dust again" (Eccles. 3:20).

Yes, "the hardest thing to give is in," to surrender. A truly Christian life requires surrender—full and absolute. We must try to commit our lives to Christ without reservation. 100 percent.

Sounds hard? It is.

When we invite the Lord into our lives, we're often reluctant to let Him *all* the way in. Sure, He can come through the door and into the living room, but please—don't look into the den—and especially not onto that top shelf in the closet! We all have a few secrets we'd like to hide—that one bad habit we're reluctant to give up.

If we're determined to be followers of Christ, we must not merely quote His commandments, we must *live* by them. We must remember that the Ten Commandments are not the "ten suggestions."

It's *hard* to give over complete control of our life to Christ. But the only way we can know that our life will be victorious is to surrender—complete and unequivocal.

"By this we know that we love the children of God, when we love God and obey his commandments" (1 John 5:2).

When tomorrow eventually becomes yesterday, as it inevitably must do, it somehow looks a little better. Our trials and tribulations never seem quite as bad in retrospect as they did at the moment we were experiencing them.

That's because at the time *we were unsure of the outcome.* (Will Uncle Melvin's operation be a success? Will the dog stay lost forever? Will my secret come out?)

We added this extra burden of worry to the load we were already carrying—an unnecessary addition because it didn't do Uncle Melvin or the dog or us any good.

If you are going to add something to your life make it something that will *lighten* your load—make it Christ. He will not only lend a helping hand, He'll willingly shoulder the entire burden, *if only you will let Him.* He waits patiently for each of us to ask Him along on our journey.

An old man was asked what had most robbed him of joy in his life. His reply was, "Things that never happened."

"This one thing I do, forgetting those things which are behind, and reaching forth unto those things which are before" (Phil. 3:13, KJV).

Even tough ol' Thelma has a need for love. How much more bearable she'd be if she'd only admit it!

It's been said of Thelma (by her fellow comic strip characters) that she "has a disposition like four bags of wet cats," and that she's "as appealing as a stroll through three acres of poison oak." Probably these descriptions are a bit exaggerated, but I'm sure she'd be a lot more popular if she'd admit to the world in general and herself in particular, that she (like everyone else) has a yearning to be loved.

Her inability to admit this basic longing makes it impossible for her to show love to others, so she finds herself trapped in an all-too-common vicious circle.

It amazes me how much mail I get from readers about Thelma—after all, she's the "heavy" of the strip. Readers request drawings of her or simply write to tell me they enjoy her. What puzzles me though, is how many of them will express a special liking for Thelma because "she reminds me of myself!" Some go on to say that Thelma does all the things they would like to do.

The world must be full of Thelmas. Reach out for one today. Show her (or him) you care.

Take a Thelma to lunch.

"Love one another as I have loved you" (John 15:12).

It's important not to confuse "wishing" with "praying." Wishing is done idly, without faith in the outcome. On the other hand, prayer is heard and considered and answered by a wise and loving God.

While God always answers prayers, we must be prepared for the fact that sometimes His answer will be *No*. When those times come—when our prayers are denied—we must know in our hearts that God, in His wisdom, is acting in our behalf *even if the reasons are incomprehensible to us*.

When we "wish" we are only talking to ourselves. When we pray, with even a tiny bit of faith, the Bible assures us that God hears and answers. If the answer is no, we have made another step in the exciting journey to discover His will.

"And we are sure of this, that he will listen to us whenever we ask him for anything in line with his will. And if we really know he is listening when we talk to him and make our requests, then we can be sure that he will answer us" (1 John 5:14,15, TLB).

Don't worry, Dooley, you caught Him in a good mood. You can count on it!

The Lord is a consistent Lord—constant in His love and in His actions. Nowhere will you find evidence of a capricious nature—of inconsistent behavior or indecision. Instead, He represents a continuing, constant source of strength and renewal.

The Rock of Gibraltar, that popular symbol of solidarity and permanence (not to mention life insurance) has been in existence but a moment, as God reckons time, and will vanish in a few more such moments. God, on the other hand, is truly eternal, here since the beginning of time and existing forever.

One of the great advantages of being a Christian is knowing that when we need the Lord for support or for forgiveness, He'll be there. As Dooley once explained to Max, "He's on duty 24 hours a day, including weekends and holidays."

"If we confess our sins, he is faithful and just, and will forgive our sins and cleanse us from all unrighteousness" (1 John 1:9).

Man, with his monumental pride, forgets that it is God, and not he who has created all things.

We herald each new discovery as a personal triumph.

We forget or don't want to admit that our "discoveries" have been there all the time, created by God and waiting to be uncovered bit-by-bit over the centuries.

We invent ever more sophisticated cameras, forgetting that each new photographic advance is but a primitive copy of some principle God has been using in the human eye all along.

We brag about our expensive electronic kidney machine, forgetting that the Lord made the original, portable unit eons ago and has been providing two free to each customer ever since.

We even take credit for the discovery of each "new" star, forgetting that God placed them all in orbit in the beginning.

Recently, the United States Patent Office issued its four millionth patent. Not one of the inventors involved ever "created" anything, they merely discovered new ways of applying or combining the material God has provided and made available to us all along.

God holds the original patent on the universe. It hasn't expired. The only royalty He receives is our love.

"For by him were all things created, that are in heaven, and that are in earth, visible and invisible" (Col. 1:16, KJV).

Almost every adult has said at some time, "Oh, to be young again and know what I know now!" There's a good chance that if we had that opportunity, we'd either make the same mistakes over or make other mistakes that would be just as disastrous.

We are constantly confronted with the necessity of making choices, not just big ones like whom to marry or what house to buy, but endless little ones like what words to say or when to step off a curb. These little decisions can have just as much effect on our lives as the "big" ones. Ask anyone who's ever stepped off a curb in front of a truck!

Without this constant stream of choices, our lives would have no real meaning.

God *gave* us our lives to live freely, even to live outside His direction if we so choose. He started by giving Adam and Eve the freedom to choose between good and evil, even though He knew in advance how disastrous that choice would be. Without that choice, however, Adam and Eve and all the billions of us who followed them would be merely exquisitely-designed robots—marionettes dangling on strings from God's fingers.

"I have set before you life and death, blessing and curse; therefore choose." (Deut. 30:19).

Noah didn't "swat both mosquitoes when he had the chance" because these lowly insects, like every other living creature, had a place in God's master plan.

What earthly good are mosquitoes? Frankly, I haven't the slightest idea. But because I'm ignorant in this area certainly doesn't mean that God pulled a boner. I'm sure He didn't put them on earth just to annoy me when I'm cutting the grass or to provide a market for the insect repellent people. No, there was a reason.

I'll confess further ignorance of entomology: I don't *really* know why butterflies are around either. I have a small one on my desk, mounted on a twig and sealed in a Lucite cube. This tiny creature (perhaps half-an-inch long) houses, among other things, a digestive system, reproductive organs, a complete optical system—and attached to either side are wings so delicate as to be completely transparent!

This once-living, breathing, self-contained flying machine wasn't built at the multi-billion dollar NASA laboratory or at one of the huge Lockheed assembly plants (neither has the know-how or facilities). It was created in the dark, in a tiny cocoon, untouched by human hand.

Let anyone who doesn't believe in God's miracles stand up and explain that one!

"How great are thy works, O Lord!" (Ps. 92:5).

IRS waiting rooms, hospital lounges and courtrooms are all scenes of a lot of prayer. More so than some churches, maybe.

The one thing these rooms have in common is that they all contain *people in trouble* or people who think they *might* be in trouble. They turn to God after all else fails and they find themselves in situations where they can't help themselves.

In circumstances like these, we might expect a lesser God to either ignore their belated requests or to reply with an exasperated, "Get lost!" But our Lord, with His limitless love, doesn't want them *lost*, He wants them *found*. Anyone who sincerely asks Christ into his life is clasped to His bosom as readily as the most devoted, lifelong disciple. God loves all people equally and without exception.

"What man of you, having a hundred sheep,
if he has lost one of them, does not leave the ninety-nine . . .
and go after the one which is lost . . .?" (Luke 15:4).

"Roughshod" is a good word to describe most of Thelma's actions. Unthinkingly, she "does unto others as she would," never seeming to be fully aware of the effect of her actions.

Like so many of us, Thelma doesn't consciously want to hurt or offend anyone. She's just so wrapped up in what *she's* doing that she's usually unaware of the feelings of anyone else.

Sure, she's heard of the golden rule. Everyone has. But like so many others, she's heard with her ears rather than with her heart and mind.

She has read the words but not the message.

Stop and think about it for a moment: if we *really* observed the golden rule, treated others as we would have them treat us, would we ever say another unkind word? Would we ever be greedy or dishonest? Indeed, would man ever declare war?

No.

The Bible has given us a short, simple formula that, if adopted, would do away with unkindness, greed, dishonesty and war.

No other book can make that statement.

"So whatever you wish that men would do to you, do so to them"
(Matt. 7:12).

105

As children in Sunday School, we all memorize the commandments, or at least we memorize the *words.* Unfortunately, memorizing the words doesn't necessarily mean we have grasped their meaning; or even come close.

We go on to memorize prayers without understanding their significance, to repeat grace by rote, and to sing hymns while thinking of yesterday's golf game or tomorrow's shopping list.

We laugh when a child prays, "Our Father who art in heaven, Harold be Thy name," or when another sings, "Gladly, the cross-eyed bear." But it's no laughing matter when an adult mechanically recites a prayer in church each week with a similar lack of comprehension, Sunday after Sunday.

Too many folks continue this perfunctory practice all through their lives. They get their mouths going but their brains aren't in gear—like cars with motors running but clutches disengaged, making noise but not getting any closer to their destination, even though they may be pointed in the right direction.

"Since their worship amounts to mere words learned by rote,
therefore I will take awesome vengeance on these hypocrites, and
make their wisest counselors as fools" (Isa. 29:13, TLB).

Has the rain ever fallen on your picnic? Or flooded the church basement? Or washed out your open-air prayer meeting?

On these occasions, it's not unusual to hear folks saying (only half in jest), "What can the Lord be *thinking* about, anyway? Why would He do this to US?

Nowhere in the Bible does the Lord promise His followers a trouble-free walk down the path of life. He doesn't promise health, wealth or days of endless sunshine.

The truth is that some of those who have the strongest belief in Christ nurture that belief from hospital beds. Some of His most devoted disciples worship Him from hovels and ghettos.

Both rain and sunshine come from the same source. If we realize this, we can accept the fact that our dark days have heavenly purpose: that all things are directed by God according to His master plan. We read in Romans 8:18, "What we suffer now is nothing compared to the glory he will give us later" (*TLB*).

Should the "just" organize? They already are! They're banding together in churches, holding rallies, forming Bible study groups, publishing books and bouncing the message of Jesus Christ off satellites to all corners of the world!

"For he maketh his sun to rise on the evil and on the good,
and sendeth rain on the just and on the unjust" (Matt. 5:45, KJV).

110

YES!

"In the world you have tribulation; but be of good cheer, I have overcome the world" (John 16:33).